Learn to Fold Origami

Backyard Wildlife

Katie Gillespie

www.av2books.com

AV² provides enriched content that supplements and complements this book. Weigl's AV² books strive to create inspired learning and engage young minds in a total learning experience.

Your AV² Media Enhanced books come alive with...

Audio
Listen to sections of the book read aloud.

Key Words
Study vocabulary, and complete a matching word activity.

Video
Watch informative video clips.

Quizzes
Test your knowledge.

Go to **www.av2books.com**, and enter this book's unique code.

BOOK CODE

J 5 0 2 3 9

Embedded Weblinks
Gain additional information for research.

Slide Show
View images and captions, and prepare a presentation.

AV² by Weigl brings you media enhanced books that support active learning.

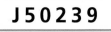

Try This!
Complete activities and hands-on experiments.

... and much, much more!

Published by AV² by Weigl
350 5th Avenue, 59th Floor
New York, NY 10118
Website: www.weigl.com   www.av2books.com

Library of Congress Control Number: 2013953157

ISBN 978-1-4896-0644-0 (hardcover)
ISBN 978-1-4896-0645-7 (softcover)
ISBN 978-1-4896-0646-4 (single user eBook)
ISBN 978-1-4896-0647-1 (multi-user eBook)

Printed in the United States of America in North Mankato, Minnesota
1 2 3 4 5 6 7 8 9 0 17 16 15 14 13

122013
WEP301113

Senior Editor: Heather Kissock
Art Director: Terry Paulhus

Every reasonable effort has been made to trace ownership and to obtain permission to reprint copyright material. The publishers would be pleased to have any errors or omissions brought to their attention so that they may be corrected in subsequent printings.

Weigl acknowledges Getty Images as its primary image supplier for this title.

Origami patterns adapted from concepts originating with Fumiaki Shingu.

Contents

6

10

14

18

22

26

3

Why Fold Origami?

Origami is the Japanese art of paper folding. The Japanese, and the Chinese before them, have been folding paper into different shapes and designs for hundreds of years. The term "origami" comes from the Japanese words "ori," which means "folding," and "kami," which means "paper."

Paper used to be very expensive, so origami was an activity that only the rich could afford. Over time, paper became less expensive, and more people were able to participate in origami. Today, it is an art form that anyone can enjoy.

It is fun to make objects out of paper. Before you start doing origami, there are three basic folds that you must learn. Knowing these three folds will help you create almost any simple origami model.

Hood Fold

Hood folds are often used to make an animal's head or neck. To make a hood fold, fold along the dotted line, and crease. Then, unfold the paper. Open the pocket you have created. Flip the paper inside out along the creases, and flatten.

Pocket Fold

Pocket folds are often used to make an animal's mouth or tail. To make a pocket fold, fold along the dotted line, and crease. Then, unfold the paper. Open the pocket you have created. Fold the point inside along the creases, and flatten.

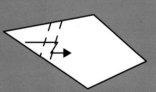

Step Fold

Step folds are often used to make an animal's ears. To make a step fold, fold backward along the dotted line, and crease. Then, fold frontward along the dotted line, and crease. Repeat as necessary.

You will need:
- Origami paper (or any square-shaped paper)
- Colored markers or crayons

Practice making your favorite backyard animals to learn the skills needed to fold origami.

Backyard Wildlife

Animals can be found all over the world. Some live in remote areas, while others live close to towns and cities. The human population is always growing. As a result, people need more houses, shopping centers, and other buildings. They expand into areas where animals once made their homes. This affects the animals' natural **habitat** and how they live.

In towns and cities across North America, people and animals now live near each other. Sometimes, people see these animals in their own backyards. Many of these animals have **adapted** to living near humans. They have developed ways of surviving in their changing environment.

As you fold the origami models in this book, think about how each animal's unique features help it to survive. Which features are most useful in a changing environment? Why?

What Is a Bat?

Bats are small, flying **mammals**. They are the only mammals capable of continued flight. Bats live all over the world, except for the North and South Poles. They are often found living in caves. There are more than 1,000 different **species** of bats.

Bats are nocturnal. This means they are mainly active at night. Bats spend much of their time looking for food. Most bats eat mosquitoes and other insects. Some eat fruit or fish. Many vampire bats survive solely on blood.

Head
Bats have large brains for their body size and are very smart. Bats can remember places and people for a long time.

Teeth
A bat's teeth are tiny but very sharp. Their jagged edges allow the bat to break through the hard shells of fruit and **prey**, such as insects.

Thumbs
Bats have thumbs that are free from their wings. They use their thumbs to help them cling to ceilings and trees.

Ears

Bats can turn their ears in the direction of sounds. At night, they use **echolocation** to find their prey. A bat will make small, high-pitched noises and wait for the noises to echo, or bounce off, other objects. Bats can find prey by listening to the echoes. The echoes also help the bats avoid flying into objects.

Fur

A bat's body is covered in fur. This fur is usually black or brown. It can also be gray, white, orange, or red.

Wings

A bat's wings are made up of two layers of skin. This skin stretches over the bat's long finger bones. It connects to the sides of the bat's body and its hind legs. The largest bats in the world have wingspans of up to 6 feet (2 meters).

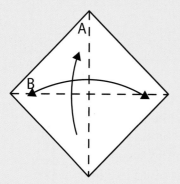

1. Fold in half along line A, and crease. Open the paper. Then, fold in half along line B, as shown.

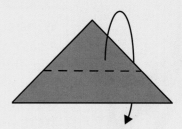

2. Fold backward along the dotted line.

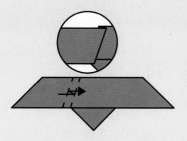

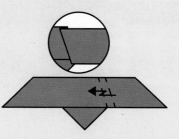

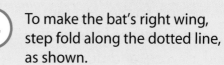

3 To make the bat's left wing, step fold along the dotted line, as shown.

4 To make the bat's right wing, step fold along the dotted line, as shown.

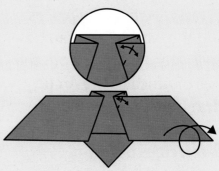

5 Fold the left point along the dotted line, and crease. Open the paper.

6 Fold the right point along the dotted line, and crease. Open the paper. Then, turn the bat over.

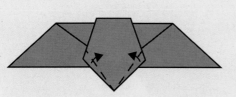

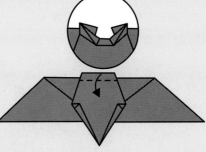

7 Fold in along the left dotted line. Then, fold in along the right dotted line.

8 Fold in along the dotted line, as shown.

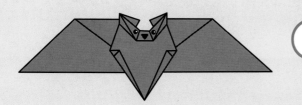

9 Finish the bat by drawing its face.

What Is a Fox?

Tail
Foxes are well known for their long, bushy tails. A fox's tail is about one-third of its body length. The tail is used for balance, communication, and warmth.

Foxes belong to the dog family. They are cousins of the wolf, jackal, coyote, and domestic dog. Foxes live in many places around the world. They can be found in areas ranging from the deserts of Africa to the Arctic **tundra**. Their habitats include grasslands, marshes, mountains, and even cities or towns.

Foxes are omnivores. This means that they eat both plants and animals. Foxes are mainly nocturnal. They hunt at night for their prey, including fish, rabbits, and birds.

Eyes

A fox's eyes are large, with oval pupils. Foxes have very good eyesight. They can see especially well in the dark. This helps them to catch their prey.

Ears

Most foxes have very large, pointed ears. They also have excellent hearing. This helps foxes catch prey moving underground.

Nose

A fox's slender nose is very sensitive to smell. Foxes use their excellent sense of smell to find prey, to tell them if other foxes are near, and to detect enemies.

Fur

Foxes use their fur to keep warm during the winter. In autumn, some foxes grow more fur to prepare for the cold. This fur changes color to match their surroundings, which helps keep the foxes hidden from **predators**. In spring, foxes shed their extra fur. During summer months, short fur protects foxes from the Sun's heat.

Paws

Foxes use their paws to dig holes. They also use them to hold down their prey. Although foxes are part of the dog family, they have cat-like claws.

How to Fold a FOX

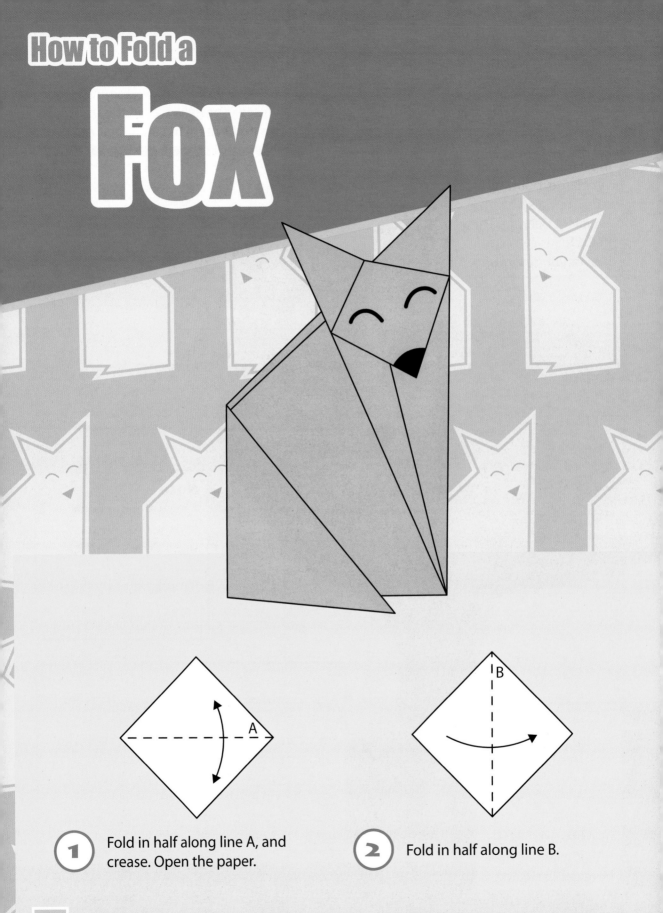

1 Fold in half along line A, and crease. Open the paper.

2 Fold in half along line B.

3 Fold the top down along the dotted line to meet the center line, as shown.

4 Fold the bottom up along the dotted line to meet the center line, as shown.

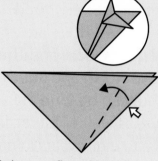

5 Fold in half backward, as shown.

6 Fold the top flap along the dotted line, as shown. Then, open the pocket at the white arrow, and flatten.

7 Turn the fox, as shown.

8 To make the fox's tail, fold the left point in along the dotted line, as shown.

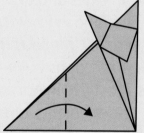

9 Finish the fox by drawing its eyes and nose.

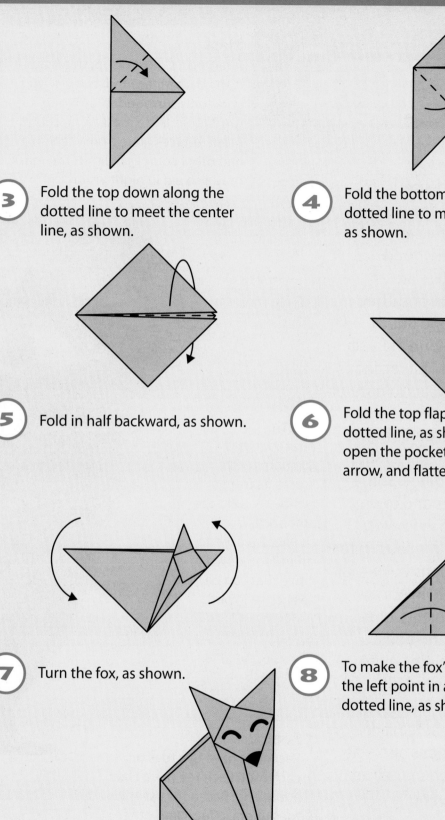

What Is a Raccoon?

R accoons are mid-sized mammals. They are intelligent, nocturnal creatures that are very good at climbing trees. There are seven species of raccoons. They are native to North and South America but can be found in Asia and Europe as well. Most raccoons live for five to eight years in nature.

The location of a raccoon's home varies. It depends on the climate and natural surroundings. Some raccoons live in cities and towns. Others can be found in forests. Raccoons generally live near water and trees. Few raccoons build their own homes. Most live in hollow tree trunks, under objects, or in abandoned lodges and dens. They move to new places quite frequently. Raccoons usually change homes every few days. They do stay in the same place during winter. Raccoons also stay in the same home when they are caring for their offspring.

Mask
A raccoon's most distinctive feature is the dark fur around its eyes. This dark fur is surrounded by white fur. It looks like a mask. A raccoon's mask reduces glare from the Sun and other sources of light. The mask may also aid in night vision.

Teeth
A raccoon has 40 sharp teeth. It uses its front, canine teeth to tear at food. Its back molars are used to grind food down to a size that can be easily swallowed.

Feet
Raccoons have five toes on each foot. Each toe has a claw at the end. Raccoons use their toes to grasp food and other objects. They also use their toes to climb trees.

Fur

Raccoons have long fur that is most often a brownish-gray color. The color of their fur helps raccoons hide from predators because it blends with their surroundings. Raccoons that live in cold climates have thicker fur than those that live in warm climates.

Tail

A raccoon's tail has five to seven dark rings. Raccoons use their tails to help them keep their balance when climbing.

Legs

A raccoon's back legs are longer than its front legs. Raccoons cannot run very fast. They waddle when they walk.

How to Fold a
Raccoon

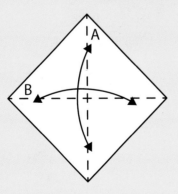

1 Fold in half along line A, and crease. Open the paper. Then, fold in half along line B, and crease. Open the paper.

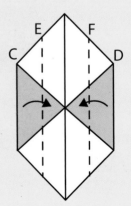

2 Fold lines C and D in to meet at the center, and crease. Then, fold lines E and F to meet at the center, and crease. Open the paper.

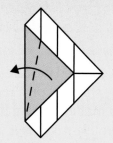

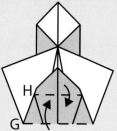
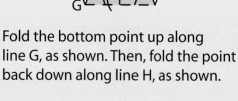

3 Fold the left point in, as shown. Then, fold along the dotted line, as shown. Repeat on the right side.

4 Fold the bottom point up along line G, as shown. Then, fold the point back down along line H, as shown.

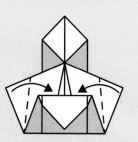

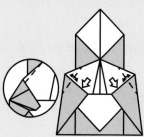

5 Fold the left side in along the dotted line, as shown. Repeat on the right side.

6 Fold along the left dotted line, and crease. Open the paper. Then, open the pocket at the white arrow, and flatten. Repeat on the right side.

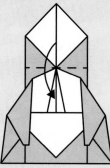

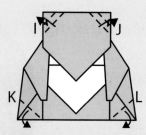

7 Fold the top point down along the dotted line, as shown.

8 To make the raccoon's left ear, step fold on line I. Repeat for line J to make the raccoon's right ear. Then, fold along dotted lines K and L, as shown.

9 Finish the raccoon by drawing its eyes, mask, and nose.

What Is a Snake?

Snakes are members of the **reptile** family. They are **cold-blooded** animals that can be found on every continent except Antarctica. There are approximately 2,900 species of snakes. Most species of snakes live between 20 and 30 years.

All snakes are carnivores. This means they eat other animals. Some snakes kill their prey by injecting them with **venom**. Others squeeze their prey to death. Once they have caught their prey, snakes swallow the food whole.

Skin

A snake's body is covered in scales. These scales overlap like shingles on a roof. A snake's scales are made from keratin, just like human fingernails. All snakes shed their skin, and a new skin takes its place. Some younger snakes shed every 20 days. Other snakes shed only once a year.

Jaw

A snake's jaw can separate from its skull. The jaw can also open at the chin. This allows the snake to swallow larger animals. After eating, the snake returns its jawbones to their normal position by yawning.

Tongue

Snakes have forked tongues. They use them, along with their **Jacobson's organ**, to help identify objects in their environment. Snakes do this by flicking their tongues out. Next, they touch their tongues to the organ to identify the scents. This tells the snake what is in its surroundings.

Teeth

Snakes have more than 200 teeth. These teeth are very sharp and point backward. This helps snakes hold onto their prey. Snakes lose their teeth often. They grow new teeth to replace them. This means their teeth are always sharp.

Eyes

Snakes do not have movable eyelids. Instead, a clear membrane covers their eyes. Snakes cannot look from side to side. They move their bodies to focus on an object that is not in front of their eyes. Snakes can see movement very well.

How to Fold a
Snake

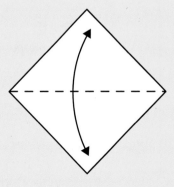

1 Fold in half along the dotted line, and crease. Open the paper.

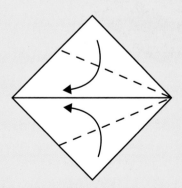

2 Fold the top down along the dotted line to meet the center line. Fold the bottom up along the dotted line to meet the center line.

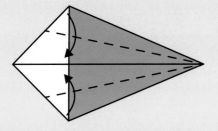

3 Fold the top down along the dotted line to meet the center line. Fold the bottom up along the dotted line to meet the center line.

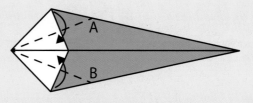

4 Fold the top point down along line A, as shown. Then, fold the bottom point up along line B.

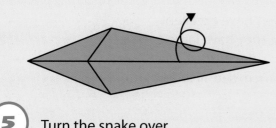

5 Turn the snake over.

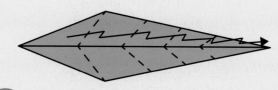

6 Step fold along the dotted lines, as shown.

7 To make the snake's head, fold along the dotted line, and crease. Then, unfold the paper and hood fold, as shown.

8 To make the snake's jaw, pocket fold at the tip, as shown.

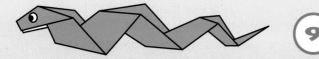

9 Finish the snake by drawing its eye.

What Is a Squirrel?

Squirrels belong to the **rodent** family. They are related to marmots, chipmunks, and prairie dogs. Squirrels can be found everywhere except Antarctica and Australia. They live in many different habitats. Squirrels make their homes in towns and cities, as well as in prairie regions, forests, deserts, and mountain areas.

There are almost 270 species of squirrels. These can be separated into three main kinds. These are ground squirrels, tree squirrels, and flying squirrels. Squirrels are omnivores. They eat nuts, seeds, and berries, as well as insects, birds, and frogs.

Eyes
Squirrels have excellent vision. They have large eyes on the sides of their head. This helps them see all around.

Teeth
All squirrels have sharp front teeth. They use their teeth to break open nuts to eat. Their teeth can also be used to defend against predators, such as eagles, foxes, wild cats, and snakes.

Paws
Squirrels use their paws to **groom** themselves. A squirrel's claws are very sharp. They use them to grip bark when climbing trees.

Tail

A squirrel's most distinctive feature is its bushy tail. The tail has several uses. On cold days, it can be used as a blanket. On a rainy day, it can act as an umbrella. If a squirrel falls from a tree, it can use its tail as a parachute. Squirrels also use their tails for balance when climbing. Squirrels often flick their tails to frighten predators.

Nose

A squirrel's nose is important for finding food. Squirrels use their keen sense of smell to locate nuts, berries, eggs, and other food.

Fur

A squirrel's fur can range in color from red or brown to gray or black. In the winter, its thick coat of fluffy fur keeps the squirrel warm by trapping a layer of air close to its body.

How to Fold a
Squirrel

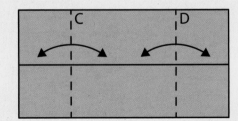

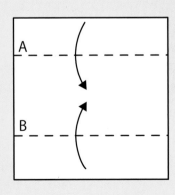

Fold along line A to meet the center, as shown. Repeat for line B.

2 Fold along line C to meet the center, and crease. Repeat for line D. Then, open the paper.

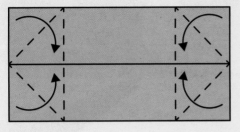

3 Fold the top right corner in along the dotted line, as shown. Repeat for the remaining three corners.

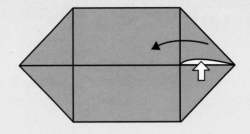

4 Open the pocket at the white arrow, and flatten. Repeat for the remaining three corners.

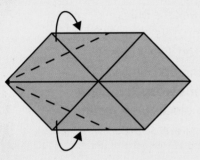

5 Fold backward along the top dotted line, as shown. Repeat for the bottom dotted line.

6 Fold along the top dotted line, as shown. Repeat for the bottom dotted line. Then, fold the squirrel in half lengthwise, as shown.

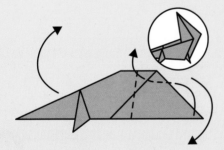

7 Fold along the dotted line, and crease. Unfold the paper. Make a pocket fold, as shown. Then, turn the squirrel.

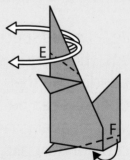

8 To make the squirrel's head, fold along line E, and crease. Then, unfold the paper and hood fold, as shown. To make the squirrel's mouth, pocket fold at the tip, as shown. Then, fold inside along line F.

9 Complete the squirrel by drawing its eye and tail pattern.

What Is a Woodpecker?

Woodpeckers are birds that are known for tapping on tree trunks with their bills. This pecking helps them find insects that live in the tree bark. It also lets them dig holes for their nests. Some woodpeckers tap to communicate with other woodpeckers, as part of their mating ritual. The average woodpecker can peck 20 times every second. Its bill strikes a tree at a speed of 12 miles (19 kilometers) per hour.

There are more than 180 species of woodpeckers. They vary in size and color, depending on their species. Woodpeckers can be found in wooded areas all over the world, except for Australia, Madagascar, and New Zealand. There are approximately 24 species in the United States. Most woodpeckers live between four and eleven years.

Bill

A woodpecker's bill is very strong. It is straight and pointed, like a chisel. To keep the tip pointed, special **cells** work to replace any worn pieces. As a result, the tip remains sharp.

Toes

A woodpecker's toes have been adapted to its life in trees. Two of the bird's toes face frontward, and two toes face backward. This arrangement lets the woodpecker move vertically on trees and poles.

Tongue

Woodpeckers have very long tongues. They measure up to 4 inches (10 cm) in length. Having a long tongue allows the woodpecker to get into places that are difficult to reach. The tip of the tongue has sharp barbs and a sticky, glue-like substance. This helps the woodpecker catch insects or grab seeds to eat.

Head

A woodpecker's skull is reinforced. When the woodpecker begins pecking, the force of the movement spreads out. This lessens the impact of the pecking and helps the woodpecker avoid headaches. Additional cushioning around the brain also helps protect the woodpecker from the force of its pecking.

Feathers

Most woodpeckers have brightly colored feathers. These feathers can be red, green, white, yellow, or brown. The feathers help to **camouflage** the birds in their habitat and hide them from predators. Woodpeckers have a pair of stiffened tail feathers. These feathers help woodpeckers to steady themselves when pecking. They press the feathers against a tree to help support their weight. Woodpeckers also have feathers over their nostrils. These bristle-like feathers stop the woodpecker from inhaling wood particles when pecking.

How to Fold a
Woodpecker

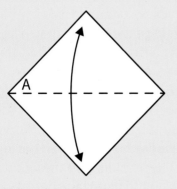

1 Fold in half along line A, and crease. Open the paper.

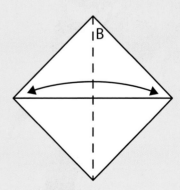

2 Fold in half along line B, and crease. Open the paper.

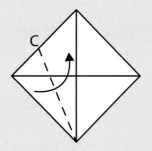

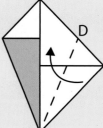

3 Fold in along line C to meet the center line.

4 Fold in along line D to meet the center line.

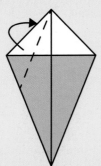

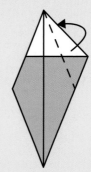

5 Fold the left side backward along the dotted line, as shown.

6 Fold the right side backward along the dotted line, as shown.

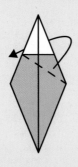

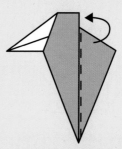

7 Fold backward along the dotted line.

8 Fold backward along the dotted line, as shown.

9 Finish the woodpecker by drawing its eye and pattern.

Test Your Knowledge of Backyard Wildlife

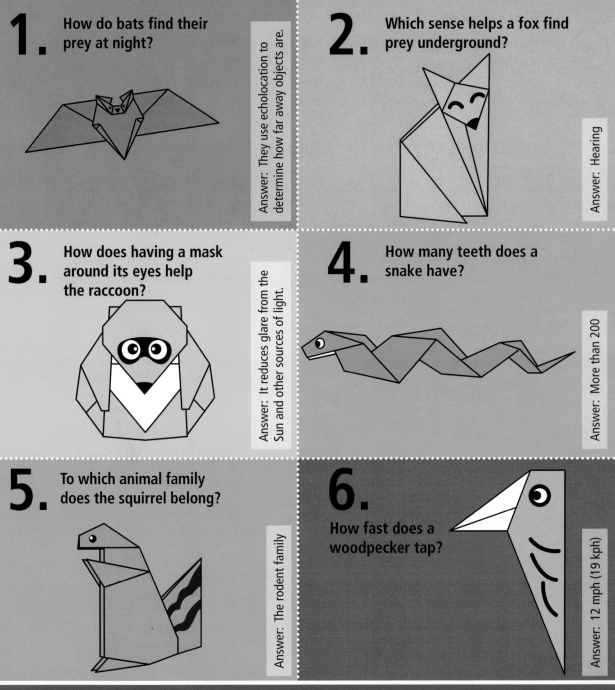

1. How do bats find their prey at night?

Answer: They use echolocation to determine how far away objects are.

2. Which sense helps a fox find prey underground?

Answer: Hearing

3. How does having a mask around its eyes help the raccoon?

Answer: It reduces glare from the Sun and other sources of light.

4. How many teeth does a snake have?

Answer: More than 200

5. To which animal family does the squirrel belong?

Answer: The rodent family

6. How fast does a woodpecker tap?

Answer: 12 mph (19 kph)

Want to learn more? Log on to www.av2books.com to access more content.

Create an Environment

Materials
- Origami paper (or any other square-shaped paper)
- Colored markers or crayons
- Tape or glue
- Large poster board
- Access to the internet or your local library

Steps
1. Choose one of the backyard animals in this book. Fold the origami model of the animal, according to the instructions.
2. Research the environment your animal lives in. You can use this book, other books from your local library, or the internet.
3. Imagine the natural surroundings where your animal makes its home. Think about the kinds of plants and animals that live there. Are there bodies of water? Is it hot and dry, or cold and snowy?
4. On your poster board, draw the features of the landscape that make up your animal's environment. Make sure you include everything you brainstormed in step 3.
5. Glue or tape your origami animal to the poster board to complete the activity. Share your work with family and friends.

Key Words

adapted: adjusted to the natural environment

camouflage: to have colors or patterns that blend in with the surroundings

cells: the basic, smallest units that can function independently in living things

cold-blooded: having a body temperature that changes with the surrounding air or water

echolocation: a method of locating objects by reflected sound

groom: make neat and pleasant in appearance

habitat: natural living place

Jacobson's organ: a patch of very sensitive cells that are part of the olfactory system in many animals

mammals: warm-blooded animals that have fur and feed milk to their babies

predators: animals that hunt and eat other animals for food

prey: an animal that is hunted for food by another animal

reptile: a type of cold-blooded animal with a backbone, lungs, and scales

rodent: a group of animals that have big front teeth

species: groups of animals or plants that share certain features

tundra: a huge plain in the Arctic that has no trees

venom: the poison of some animals

Log on to www.av2books.com

AV² by Weigl brings you media enhanced books that support active learning. Go to www.av2books.com, and enter the special code found on page 2 of this book. You will gain access to enriched and enhanced content that supplements and complements this book. Content includes video, audio, weblinks, quizzes, a slide show, and activities.

AV² Online Navigation

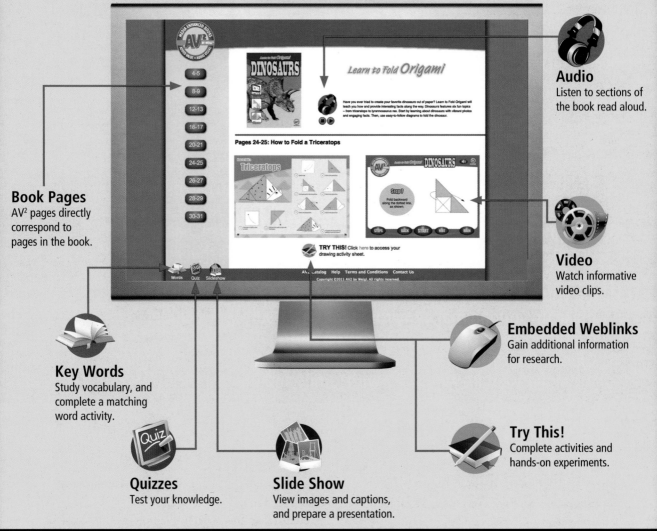

Audio
Listen to sections of the book read aloud.

Book Pages
AV² pages directly correspond to pages in the book.

Video
Watch informative video clips.

Embedded Weblinks
Gain additional information for research.

Key Words
Study vocabulary, and complete a matching word activity.

Try This!
Complete activities and hands-on experiments.

Quizzes
Test your knowledge.

Slide Show
View images and captions, and prepare a presentation.

AV² was built to bridge the gap between print and digital. We encourage you to tell us what you like and what you want to see in the future.

Sign up to be an AV² Ambassador at www.av2books.com/ambassador.